The Free Spirit
God in Us

The Free Spirit

God in Us

Gabriele

Gabriele
Publishing House

First Edition, December 2016
Published by:
© Gabriele Publishing House
THE WORD
Max-Braun-Str. 2 – 97828 Marktheidenfeld – Germany

Translated from the original German title:
Der Freie Geist
Gott in uns
Order No. S 179ENPOD

The German edition is the work of reference for all
questions regarding the meaning of the contents

.

ISBN 978-3-89201-793-6

Table of Contents:

Foreword

There is a lot of talk about God and a lot is written – but who knows the truth?
The fact is that no person can prove to another that God exists. Nor can any external religion, any church institution, provide the proof that God truly exists.

But in this book we read: God in us!
Who can say such a thing?
A person who experiences God in herself. It is Gabriele, the prophetess and emissary of God in our time, who lives in God and has been giving humankind His word of truth for 40 years. In this book, Gabriele gives food for thought, impulses and aids, so that each person can prove for himself that God exists and that He dwells in us.

And so, each person can experience God for himself, thus gaining the joy and certainty that God is in each one of us. God is in all life forms. God is present in all things.

The basis for this book is four television programs entitled "Your Devotional – The Free Spirit. God in Us," in which several followers of Jesus of Nazareth participated. The content of the programs is given by Gabriele, who, as the emissary of the Free Spirit, gives the truth to all God-seeking people from her rich treasury of experience and from the horn of plenty of divine Wisdom.
The program texts have been edited for this written version and are passed on in this book.

"God in Us" shows the reader the path to freedom, out of confining religious beliefs, out of rigid traditions, out of binding institutions – toward God, toward God in us.

Gabriele Publishing House – the Word

The topic "God in Us" is a provocation for many people in our time. When you read and listen via the media about what is becoming apparent in this world, the word GOD slips more and more into the background, to say nothing of the statement "God in Us"!

We hear about the disasters in this world and how people are acting toward their fellow humans, that is, how they treat their own kind, how they live in enmity with those who do not share their views. The Earth with its animals and plants suffers under the fraudulent labeling "Christian" – which means: "We do what Jesus taught" – under the egoism of exploitation. With countless arguments, the Earth is plundered; the animals are tortured and killed and nature is run down. Certainly, all this has nothing to do with God and Jesus.

And now someone comes who claims: "God in us."

"God in us" is actually not an abstract term. Above all, it should not be an abstract term, if we believe in Jesus of Nazareth, in the Christ of God, who – as Christians say – is the Redeemer of humankind.

One of His many teachings stands as a reminder. Jesus taught us that every person is the temple of God and that God, the Eternal, dwells in each one of us. So "God in us" is not an abstract term if we believe in Jesus, the Christ, in His teaching, yes, in His simple teachings.

Unfortunately, we human beings are very warped in our thinking. We believe in church institutions that celebrate their rigmarole in the name of "Christian." However, Jesus of Nazareth did not bring us any cult teachings. Instead, you, each and every one of us, are the temple of God and God dwells in every person, in every soul.

Recently, many people have been thinking about this and many, yes, ever more people, are leaving the church institutions. We hear more and more about the debaucheries committed by the caste of priests, about hypocrisies, lies, and not lastly, about countless perversities and excesses that we don't even want to call by name, unless we talk about ugliness and abnormality.

Let us remember Jesus of Nazareth, the Christ of God, who rightly said: *But you are not to be called rabbi, for you have one teacher, Christ, and you are all brothers.*
This applies, above all, to the ecclesiastical excellencies and eminences, to the entire caste of priests. Every person is more or less a sinner, including the priests.

If we believe in the words "God in us," then for each of us, the question is: Do we really need churches of stone?

God, our eternal Father, already said through Isaiah: *The Most High does not dwell in temples made by hands …*
Every churchgoer should ask himself: "Where shall I go to pray?"

Let us take the words of Jesus: *You are the temple of God, and God dwells in you* – in all of us. Then this means that we should seek out our temple of flesh and bone in the profound understanding of "God in us."
If God is in us, for what do we need priests, whom Jesus called Rabbi? Besides, Jesus, the Christ, taught us that the Kingdom of God is within, in us. Then why should we go to churches of stone, if the Kingdom of God is in us and God dwells in us?

God is the law of life, and the law of life is freedom, because God is freedom and dwells in us. And so: God in us.

Christian means:
to follow the teachings
of Jesus of Nazareth

Many people – and it's ever more people – hardly find a hold in the stone churches. That's why the number of people leaving the church is increasing. Many are disappointed by the institutional behavior of the priests, and by the Doctors of the church. Many no longer feel at home in the churches of stone, because they did not find God there. Others simply shake their head, saying: "There is no God. If there were one, where is he then?"

Church authorities are no longer credible and political parties whisper about the common good and social welfare. When we look deeper, we see that it's mainly about dividends, about their own welfare. The politicians in the so-called "Christian" parties govern the German people in a country that is the world's third largest arms exporter. But they call themselves Christian!

However, Christian means to follow the teachings of Jesus of Nazareth.

When we hear that Germany is the third-largest arms exporter in the world – why does one then call oneself Christian? Is the so-called "Christian" government dependent on the church institutions? This certainly cannot be Christian! Jesus, the Christ, told us something entirely different: *All who take the sword will perish by the sword.*

And He also taught: *Love your enemies. Do good to those who hate you.*

And: *Blessed are the meek … for they shall inherit the earth.*

Jesus further taught: *As you did it to one of the least of these my brothers, you did it to me.*

Basically, the teaching of Jesus of Nazareth is the teaching of nonviolence. He did not say that we should arm ourselves to strike back. He taught us:

If anyone strikes you on the right cheek, turn to him the other also.

To let yourself be struck on a cheek and to turn the other cheek is one of those things. How could we examine this more closely according to the law of God? It could be thought that such a person will put up with anything. Is that correct according to the law of God?

Here, too, Jesus was a role model for us. When Jesus was arrested to be taken before Pontius Pilate, an officer struck Him in the face and Jesus asked: *Why do you strike me? If I have spoken wrongly, bear witness to the wrong; but if I have spoken rightly, why do you strike me?*

Jesus merely set the record straight. He stood up for the truth, but He did not strike back.

So, this means that we should not put up with everything, but should ask – as Jesus taught us: *Why are you treating me this way?*

But if Germany is the third-largest arms exporter, then this means that it approves attacking other countries with these arms and thereby killing people. This means that you attack or hit back.

Why a Christian government, if what Jesus taught is not heeded? Or is this government a backer of the caste of priests in Germany, whose law and justice is conflict, the fight against the neighbor?

That it is as it is, is evinced by the church institutions with annual subsidies in Germany amounting to about 14 billion Euros. As long as it stays this way, not very much will change, because the state horse doesn't even think it's necessary to throw off its dogmatic church rider and to change its behavior toward God and His Son, Christ.

Where is God?

For this reason, over and over again the question: What do we want with God, to say nothing of "God in us"? If God allows all this, then it would have to be said: There is no God. And if there were one, why does He allow all that? Where is He, if He is supposedly All-wise?

Perceptive scientists, atomic physicists and quantum physicists have meanwhile recognized that God is not separate from His creation, but that God is omnipresent in creation. And so, if He is omnipresent in His creation, then He is also in us. Therefore: God in us.

God, the omnipresent Spirit, is freedom. According to the will of God, every person is free, and is responsible for what he does and does not do. Even when a person drapes a Christian cloak around himself, but underneath reviles the Christian life, the free Spirit will not intervene, because every person is free and is the architect of his own fortune or misfortune. We human beings have received the teachings from God, the Eternal, and from His Son, Jesus, which would make us free if we would live accordingly. We human beings have the Ten Commandments of God through Moses, and anyone who calls himself Christian ought to also fulfill the teachings of Jesus of Nazareth, because the commandments of God are also contained in His Sermon on the Mount.

We may not forget that at the end of the Sermon on the Mount, Jesus taught us the following:

Everyone then who hears these words of mine and does them will be like a wise man who built his house on the rock. And the rain fell, and the floods came, and the winds blew and beat on that house, but it did not fall, because it had been founded on the rock.

And everyone who hears these words of mine and does not do them will be like a foolish man who built his house on the sand. And the rain fell, and the floods came, and the winds blew and beat against that house, and it fell, and great was the fall of it.

Many people build on sand. Jesus essentially said that when the water masses come, they will be washed away with the sand. We people have the spiritual principles of God from God-Father and His Son, Christ. Who lives according to them? If, despite this knowledge, we build on sand, then we should not blame God for the misfortune that hits us. God leaves us our freedom. God does not coerce. In the Commandments of God, it says "you shall," but not you must. In this is given the freedom for a free decision and ultimately, also the responsibility for every individual who knows about the commandments of God and the Sermon on the Mount of Jesus.

And so, the responsibility for each one of us lies in the "you shall." Either we do the will of God, or if we don't do it, then each one bears the responsibility for himself. If we believe in Jesus of Nazareth – even if it is only some aspects of His teachings – and we don't do what is from God's law, then ultimately we ourselves are responsible for our actions and cannot hold anyone else responsible. Whether we believe in God or not, God is in us.

Let's get back to our world, to the great poverty in our world. Children are starving; people are living in conditions that are beneath human dignity, and the "Christian" governments affirm and even contribute to the fact that churches and cathedrals are restored with countless millions of Euros. In the end, to all intents and purposes, this is raised by the state, that is, by us, the citizens. But what could be done in our world with all these countless millions? Why do we need restored churches and cathedrals, if God is not in a church of stone, but dwells in us, and God is also in every child that starves to death?

We have to become aware and try to grasp in our hearts the meaning of: God in us.

God in you.
God in each one of us.
The mighty, omnipresent God.
The omnipresent God is in every animal, in the blade of grass, in the flower, in the mighty tree, in every stone is God.

The power of life, the power of the Earth, all in all things is the omnipresent life, it is God in us, God in all things.
God is the Free Spirit, and therefore you, we, each one of us, is responsible for his or her own life.
A wise man, who does not build on sand, is aware that he, himself, is the temple of God.

He says: "I build my life on the Spirit of God and, step by step, I live the commandments of God and the Sermon on the Mount of Jesus, because God is in me."

Let us remember God's words through the prophet Isaiah:

The Most High does not dwell in temples made by human hands. …

When we continue with our topic "God in us," we understand ever better what it means, God in us, and each one of us is the temple of God, and God, the almighty, omnipresent power, dwells in us. When we go for a walk, God is in everything, because He is omnipresent. This means: communication with the life, which is God.

Our world shows us that most of us believed in the caste of priests. However, if what the priests have been proclaiming for thousands of years were the truth, then the state of this world would be different. But the condition

of our world shows us who we human beings are: war, murder, manslaughter, hunger,
suffering, disease, pestilence, animal torture
without end, and then we ask:
Where is God?

In any case, not in a house of stone that calls
itself a church, nor in the doctrines of the caste
of priests. Anyone who refers to the teachings
of Jesus, the Christ – and the caste of priests
also does this in its churches of stone – should
actually be a peaceable, God-conscious person, who cherishes the Earth and everything
that lives in it, on it and over it, and shows
respect for the life.

And so, there is no God of the priests, but
there is *the* God, the true God in you, in us,
in all people, in all creatures of God, in all of
creation, in all of nature.
A loud sound is becoming ever louder: "Why
does God allow all this"?

Well, what should God do with the all-too-human pile of shards? Should He smash it to pieces? Should He grind it up? God doesn't need to do this; we human beings already do it ourselves, because we are the ones who have made this world and the Earth into what it is, not God.

God gave us free will, because the life, which is God, is free. God does not coerce. He coerces no creature. God is freedom. God is the Spirit of life. Anyone who wantonly destroys the life is against God and puts himself above the mighty Spirit – God.

*The one who thinks freely
is a good analyst*

The freedom from God enables us to think freely.

Several questions for a good analyst and for all those who are now shaking their head:

Are you a herd animal and a yes-man? Are you a person who believes what people lead other people to believe, also when this or that one talks about God? Are you the herd animal that needs a church of stone and traditions and denominations and thus, dogmatic priests?

Or are you a free spirit, who has learned to weigh and measure, and does not believe everyone who tries to make you believe something – even if it is the promise that God is here and there, or even that the chaos of this world is a mystery of God?

Why, actually, do the institutions, but also individual people, keep talking about the "mystery of God"?

Let us ask ourselves: Is God perfect, that is, is He the absolute Spirit? If He is the absolute Spirit, the Spirit of creation, the Spirit of freedom, the Spirit of infinity, why does He need a mystery? Does God have to hide something from us human beings? If that were true, then, for one thing, the Eternal One would not be free, and for another, He would also be a sinner, because only a sinner has to hide something. Only the sinner has his mysteries, but not God.

Who coined the mystery and who wants to instill this in us? It was not Jesus of Nazareth. Whatever you may read in the Bible, Jesus never spoke of a mystery. The mystery is an invention of the priests who, bit by bit, veiled and darkened the teachings of Jesus of Nazareth, and everything that as a result was no longer logical, is passed off to their faithful as a mystery of God.

*A follower of Jesus of Nazareth
tells of his experience*

"Being aware of God in me, I let go of believing in the priests and I learned to pray again and again to God in me, and, step by step, to fulfill in my daily life what I pray. I also learned to question myself as to whether what I think, speak and do corresponds to the teachings of Jesus of Nazareth. If not, then I strive to rectify, step by step, my all-too-human aspects, this sinfulness, with the power of the inner being. Through this, I become freer, happier and from within, much easier in my mind.

I can go into nature, I can pray in nature, and realize over and over again that whatever I see, I feel in myself, because God, the free Spirit, the mighty Creator, is in everything.

In time, we learn to communicate with the forces *in* nature, with the forces in the animal and not lastly with the forces of infinity, for God is the Spirit of infinity.

I can say that I am becoming ever freer. I can pray freely; I no longer need to merely believe in a God of love, of unity, of peace and freedom. In deep prayer, I experience God in me."

What is community spirit?

According to our inner predispositions, we are communal people. No one should be alone, for it is said: It is not good for a person to be alone. But this does not mean to run after a person. Anyone who strives to find God in himself simultaneously develops the real, true community spirit.

What do we understand under community spirit?

A true and alive community spirit should actually have an inner relationship with God. From the living faith of the individual grows a deep friendship to one another, a genuine communality.

A genuine communality also develops when the one openly tells the other what is still not in order with him. If his fellowman subsequently recognizes his aspects of disorder and clears them up, then this results in a genuine, open friendship, because they practice straightforwardness, in which any kind of ulterior disparagement of the other has no place.

And so, to find God and to develop a real, deep community spirit, an inner friendship, an open, honest communality means to first find ourselves in the awareness of what Jesus, the Christ, taught the people. Among other things, He taught us: *I, Christ, Am the way, the truth and the life; no one comes to the Father except through Me.*

When we take the words of Jesus, the Christ, seriously and apply them in daily life, then we experience ever more deeply that the human being is not an individual being, but a communal being.

In the Kingdom of God, from where we all originated in the very basis of our souls, there are no individual beings, no loners. They have extended families there, and in their midst, God-Father, who, according to the principle of unity, is Mother and Father to each divine being. So, in the Kingdom of God, as well, a community spirit is totally regarded as a matter of course.

We speak of community spirit. In the Kingdom of God, one speaks of extended families, whose members are all equally permeated and carried by God, the power of the universe. And so, we can conclude, in turn, unity, equality, freedom, brotherliness, the same as brotherli- sisterliness. Each one is oriented toward the great light – God.

A person who promises something should also be able to prove it, particularly when it has to do with the divine laws. Many people – above all priests – think that they can prove God. But no person can prove God to someone else.

Each person must find God for himself. And where can He be found? He is within, in every single one. A person who has turned to God may very well tell about his experience on how he grew closer to God in himself, but he cannot prove that to others.

It has meanwhile become totally clear to me, that is, I have learned that God cannot be found here or there; God is the life, the power in us, in each one of us.
I learned early on that I do not bind myself to any person, not even when he promises me a lot, and wants to lead me here and there in order to reach God. I am aware that I alone must find God, for God is in me. If I take the

path "God in me," then I find the way to myself, my inner self, and also to my neighbor, who is my brother and sister, who also walks the path to God in him or herself. This is the one and true path: God in us, which brings people together, which lets people find their way to each other. Everything else, if we think the nearness to God can be attained here and there, is deceptive.

So, this means that even when a person has found his way to God in his innermost being, he cannot prove it to another. A good role model can be an indication, but not proof.

Consequently, words from the truth are never binding, because they contain the teachings of Jesus, the Christ. He gave us the promise, by which we should abide: *I,* thus speaks Christ, *Am the way, the truth and the life.* And He, Christ, is one with God, His Father and ours. So, our concern should be to find our way to God in us, each one for himself. Then we will be guided into the community that likewise takes this path. Each one follows this path himself. Why? Because each one has his own hurdles to overcome. Each one has inflicted other burdens, other sins, upon himself, which, step by step and with God in himself, he remedies and clears up, so that he may become free of disorder, and find his way to the Order of God, to His law of life. The teachings of Jesus give us the orientation, so that we may find our way into the community in His Spirit, to a true, genuine friendship with those people who do that, which God in us wants.

We live in the great ocean GOD

In the great work of revelation "This Is My Word. Alpha and Omega. The Gospel of Jesus. The Christ-Revelation, which True Christians the World Over Have Come to Know," we read that Jesus of Nazareth was already confronted by His contemporaries with questions about God. We can read there:

And some who were full of doubt came to Jesus, saying, "You told us that our life and being are from God, but we have never seen God, nor do we know of any God. Can You show us the One whom You call the Father and the only God? We do not know whether there is a God."

Jesus answered them, saying, "Hear this parable about the fishes. The fishes of a river spoke with one another and said: They tell us that our life and being comes from water, but we have never seen water, we do not know what it is. Then some of them, who were wiser than the others, said: We have heard that a wise and learned fish who knows all things lives in the sea. Let us go to him and ask him to show us the water.

And so, some of them set out to search for the great and wise fish, and they finally came to the sea where the fish lived, and they asked him.

And when he heard them, he said to them: Oh, you foolish fish, that you do not think. Yet wise are the few of you who seek. You live and move in water and have your existence in the water; you have come from the water and you will return to the water. You live in the water, but you do not know it. In the same way, you live in God and yet you ask Me: Show us God. God is in all things and everything is in God."

We could ask ourselves:
How do we think?
Where do we seek God?
Is not God the life in all things and in everyone?

We live in the great stream of life, which encompasses elements, nature, animals and people, and yet, often we do not know where our Creator is, the Creator of heaven and of Earth, the Creator of nature, of the animals – God is in all things.

An essential step is taken when we no longer seek, but become aware that everything is the great unity, which is: GOD.

We should become aware that the stream of life is God.

Let us practice to comprehend:

God in infinity.

God in heaven. God on Earth. God in the elements, in nature, in each blade of grass. God in every animal and God in us.

If the substance of this thought draws ever closer to us, if it seizes us at our level of feelings, we will gradually sense that we are not separated from the great ocean of life. Then we will become aware that ultimately, symbolically spoken, we live in the water of life and consciously move in the water of the Being, in the great ocean, God.

If we then immerse in the ocean God, in the water of life, by doing, step by step, what *God* wants, namely, to keep His commandments and to apply the teachings of Jesus, then we will also find our way to the community spirit, of which it is said: the inner predisposition of the person is the solidarity of those of like mind in God.

As soon as we feel the connection with the stream of life, we very gradually feel that we are not alone. If, in the community of "God in us," we walk *the* path that Jesus taught us over and over again, that is, which Jesus wanted to give us an understanding of, then we understand His word that He, Christ, is the way, the truth and the life.

And, when we follow His teachings step by step, then we find our way to people who also think and live similarly. From this, develops the true, genuine, deep community spirit that is free of the binding of the one to the other, but, in their inner beings, are all profoundly linked with God.

When we really think about the statement "God in us," the objection could arise: "What a statement! When we look at today's society, it's presumptuous to say such a thing!" But in many of the Bibles used by priests it truthfully says: … *the Most High does not dwell in houses made by human hands* … This raises the question: "Where then does God dwell, if not in churches of stone?"

Most people are familiar with the idea that in them lives a soul. We could now philosophize about whether this is true or not.

But let's just assume as a given, that we are vivified by a finer material body, which is not from this world. Let's assume that deep in the very basis of the soul, in this finer substance, is the life, the breath of life, God, whom we experience in our breathing.

The fact of "life" should not be seen as limited to only the earthly shell, the person, who at some point, breathes out and does not bring the breath back again by inhaling.

The life is eternity, and we call eternity, God, or Eternal One or eternal existence or eternal Being.

Let's just think of nature. Spring brings more light, more sun. And the part of the Earth that has turned to the sun comes alive. Nature begins to turn green and to blossom.

What is it like with us? When we turn to the light, God in us, our soul becomes more light-filled; we live more consciously and become freer and happier. We become honest, open, straightforward and just toward our fellow-man, because we have found ourselves in God, the life, and are true to ourselves.

And the one who is true to himself is also true to others, which means he does not betray them; he does not deceive or lie to them. He speaks the truth, even when it is disagreeable to the one he faces. But a true friend, who speaks the truth himself, appreciates the truth and may even gain a pointer from it, for finding the way into the depths even more, into the All-truth.

Let's get back to our topic: God in us – God in you – God in me, and that each one of us is the temple of God and that God dwells in us. So, the immortal life, the breath of God, is in the very basis of our soul. The life flows through our soul; it flows into our cell body and we breathe the life. Our heart beats, because it receives the life from the all-encompassing life, God.

If you would like to, try it out.

Each day, at every moment, we can learn to draw closer to God, the life in us, and we can practice perceiving the life, God, which surrounds us in all things. Then we experience God. We experience God and no longer bind ourselves to people who pretend they can prove God.

God is freedom

Whoever has become convinced that God, the All-Spirit, is in all things and in everyone no longer needs any external religions; nor does he need any churches of stone or priests, ceremonies and dogmas. He strives for the free Spirit, Christ in us, in every person, in every soul. Free from external religions, the liberated soul and the person take a deep breath and a previously unimagined joy over the freedom attained lends wings to our life from then on. It is God in us, God in you, God in each one of us.

Each of us is the temple of God and God dwells in us. So, is the immortal life, God – God in us – the breath? Is His life also in the very basis of *our* soul?

Oh yes, the life flows through our soul. It flows in our body of cells. And we breathe the life. Our heart beats because it receives the life, the radiating power from the all-encompassing life, God. And what is it like when, while dying, while taking our last breath, we breathe out and do not breathe in again? Then the life has withdrawn from our body. Where is the life now? Is it then extinguished? Or does it continue? It continues, because when the person exhales, at the very same moment the soul inhales.

For many priests and pastors, "God in us" is something abstract, because priests and pastors base themselves on churches of stone and on traditions.
But Jesus of Nazareth did not teach us any church traditions. Jesus did not teach us that we should go into stone temples, to perhaps find God there. Jesus taught something else, and back then He also said this to the priests, and it was true back then and is still true today: *But you are not to be called Rabbi, for you have one teacher, Christ …*

Jesus said: *You have one teacher.* So we could ask: Where is the teacher? It is Christ, the resurrection and the life *in us*. Thus, the Christ of God is the Christ of God in us. In God, He is the law of love and of freedom.

So, you, like all people, are free either to believe or not to believe, to bind yourself or to become free. You are free to go into stone churches and to follow church traditions. But just as freely, you can become aware that God does not know any traditions. God does not dwell in stone temples. It is: God in us. Everyone is himself the temple of God. This awareness lets us sense ever more deeply that God is omnipresent.

No person should pretend to another something that he cannot prove, particularly when it concerns: God in us.

No person should bind others to traditions and church prayers, to organ music and choral singing, to church rites or forms.

Try to grasp that with God there is none of this. God dwells in you. God dwells in each one of us.

We human beings always want proof. For example, a reader could think: "We may very well say 'God in me,' 'God in everything,' 'God is omnipresent.' But is this true? Can you prove it?" No person can prove this to another person. But we can plainly and simply say: Try it out for yourself! God is in you and He lets Himself be found.

Many people have already tried it out – in prayer, in the devotion: God in us. The one who does not let up in his fervent striving to find God in himself, by actualizing step-by-step the commandments of God and the teachings of Jesus of Nazareth, will gradually sense God in himself – God in all of us.

Nearness to God makes us happy. Soon we notice that we can live a meaningful life only with those people who walk the same path

– "God in us." From this truly grows the community spirit, the community life, the true, genuine, deep friendship. It develops only when it is: God in us; God in our neighbor; God *for* us and we for God.

A true life is the life in God

Jesus of Nazareth taught us to go into a quiet chamber and to seek God in the stillness. He did not teach us to go into stone churches. How can we follow this advice about a quiet chamber? For instance, in my home I have set up a little prayer corner, with a small table, a chair and a candle. In time, it became a concern of my heart to withdraw, in order to pray or to attune myself through music, to become quiet, and then direct several deep and fervent prayers to within, to God in us.

Try it out. Set up a simple prayer corner. Through music and prayer, let it become a place that attracts you more and more. And realize, over and over again, that God, our heavenly Father, loves you; He loves all of us. He wants us to go to Him, because in the very basis of our soul, we are all children, sons and daughters of the Kingdom of God. The King-

dom of God is our true, our everlasting home
– eternally.

Jesus taught us: The Kingdom of God is within,
in you. In other words, the Kingdom of God is
the law of life; it is God. Consequently, God is
in us.

Each one is free to believe or not, that as a
human being he is merely a wayfarer, who
bears eternity in himself. For the existence in
this world, our soul has temporarily taken on
a human body. Once the physical body passes
on, then the soul continues its path in the
spheres of the beyond. And it will keep going
on this path until it has completely found its
way into its inner being again, to its Creator, to
God, its Father. And then it is one with Him. As
Jesus said of Himself: *My Father and I are one.*
Wonderful words of Jesus, the Christ: My Father and I are one. – Ultimately, this is the goal
for each and every one of us. We come from
God; we are in God and we will again walk the

path to God in us, so that we again become one with the mighty stream, with the immeasurable ocean of the All-Being, God in us. Then as pure beings, we too, may say: My Father and I are one.

This prospect could lend us wings. Only the inner unity in God, our eternal Father, links us as brothers and sisters who belong to the Kingdom of God. Only the eternal homeland in God, our Father, unites us.

Let us briefly return to the term "community spirit." Community with our neighbor, who, like us, is a son or daughter of the Infinite, links us with God, our Father, and with the eternal homeland. That is where the path leads to. That is the life. The true life is the life in God. And a life pleasing to God is the truth. And, in the last analysis, the truth is the Kingdom of God.

We hope and wish that you have also become aware that no external organization can lead you to God. It's true that there are external communities, but when we adhere to the words "external community," then the question arises: Is there a true, genuine friend, who has the perseverance and the charisma to carry each individual according to the inner community?

At some point, each person must find himself. For this reason, we may encourage you to self-discovery, with the questions: Who are you? Who are we really?

Everyone who wants to will find his way to himself. And everyone who wants to will analyze the meaning of the following:

> God is always present.
> He is the infinity.
> He is in the cosmos, the All.
> He is in nature, in each animal,
> in each plant, in each stone.
> He is in the elements.
> He is in the human being.
> God is omnipresent.

If these words have also awakened in you a longing for God in us, then you, and all of us, can seek this nearness to God again and again. If we orient ourselves to the quiet chamber, then, again and again, we will be attracted by this place – be it merely a quiet corner in our room.

Let us keep this small area, arranged for collecting ourselves internally and for contemplation, free of bad, all-too-human thoughts, and let us withdraw to this familiar corner only when we want to listen to tranquil music and go into prayer. And when we pray, then let us pray deeply into the very basis of our soul, that is, to within, because we ourselves are the temple of God and God dwells in us. What we, followers of Jesus, the Christ, want is to bear witness to God, not for us, not for a traditional community, but solely for God. We want to give our fellowman an understanding of Him.

We have found God, the life, deep in our soul and we know that He loves us all, because as our eternal Father, He beheld and created us in His heart. And whoever seeks a connection to Him in deep prayer, will sense Him more and more. We can talk about this, but we cannot prove it to anyone.

We know, and yet we cannot prove:
You, all of us, live eternally, because God is eternal. He, God, our heavenly Father, created us as pure, fine-material beings. At some point, our body will pass on, but His call holds true, for example, through the words of the Christ of God, which say: *Come to me* – that is, to Christ – *all who labor and are heavy-laden and I* – that is, Christ – *will give you rest.*

And so, where should we go, when the Spirit of God, the Christ of God, dwells in the very basis of our soul, after all?
To Him, who dwells in us, to God in us.

How can we grow closer to God?

People frequently ask: "Where should we go, when the Spirit of God, the Christ of God, really does dwell in the very basis of our soul? How can we reach Him?"

The Christ of God in Jesus of Nazareth gave us a wonderful path that leads inward to the very basis of our soul. It is the communication of the heart, by way of which each person can build a living connection to the eternal Spirit within.

If you want to have this God-experience, then absorb the following words of Jesus of Nazareth in your awareness:

But when you pray, go into your room and shut the door and pray to your Father who is in secret. And your Father who sees in secret will reward you!

Jesus spoke of a quiet room; we speak of a "quiet chamber."

It would be advisable to seek out a quiet chamber – today perhaps we would say, a prayer corner or a quiet place in a room – to go within, to collect ourselves, so that we put more and more order in our thoughts and thus, become still. This is the way to detach ourselves from our all-too-human thoughts. Ultimately, it is a step toward positive thinking.

Withdraw to a quiet corner, to reflect about what the following means:

God is always present.

God is in nature. God is in each animal and in every plant, in every stone, in every mighty tree.

God is in the very basis of your soul.

God is with you and by you.

God is above you, in the mighty stars and planets. Everywhere is the all-ruling Spirit, whom we people in the western world call GOD.

That would be the first step, to realize that God is always present. And the second step would be: If God is always present in all of nature, in every animal, then logically, He must also be in you, in the very basis of your soul.

If you should have difficulties with the quiet chamber, then think about Jesus of Nazareth. He taught us that every person is the temple of God and that the Spirit of infinity, whom we call God, dwells in the person, in each soul. What do you, what do all of us, want to do with these statements? Simply push them aside? Or perhaps think about them briefly? Even if just for a brief moment, our thoughts will go ever deeper and we will reflect longer and longer about it, and suddenly we feel: Something in us wants to be fulfilled. What? It is prayer.

So light a candle. Sit up straight and pray to within, to the very basis of your soul. If your emotions are agitated and if you don't calm down, then listen to some harmonious music. This will help you cast off your thoughts from the day and will attune you for going within, to pray deeply.

In time, you will recognize that during these minutes, you enter your own inner world and sense yourself in a completely new way. In this way, you learn to find your way to yourself. Very soon, you will feel that you are not alone, that a great, mighty Spirit, the power of infinity, dwells in you. He gives you help and strength, not only to pray, but also to master your daily life in His Spirit.

At some point, the question will come up in you, as in all of us: What more can I, can we do, to grow closer to God, to change our whole basic attitude, our entire way of life toward the positive? When this desire of our heart sounds out, we will remember the divine gifts that are already given to us as a guide. We have received the Ten Commandments from God, our eternal Father, through Moses, and from Jesus, the Christ, the Sermon on the Mount.

Again and again, we hear that positive thinking is of value. And many a one asks: What actually is positive thinking?

We could say, for instance: "I affirm that the person is good." Or: "I enjoy being in nature, hearing the twittering of the birds. I affirm my day's work and am largely in accord with my colleagues at work." Now, are all these positive thoughts? Or are there still other aspects to consider than mere external affirmation?

One help for your self-help could be to figure out for yourself:

What is behind my so-called positive thoughts, words and actions? Is it all through and through good and irreproachable? Or aren't there totally different kinds of feelings and thoughts hidden behind many of these seemingly positive thoughts and behavior patterns?

Perhaps we secretly disparage our fellowman or exploit him.

For example, I now speak or act in such a way that my neighbor assents and does for me what I can't do so well. I will talk well, using flattering words, so that he takes over part of my work. Can we then call this positive? Outwardly, it does sound as though it's positive. But the content of our behavior patterns, what we conceal from the others as much as possible, has a completely different veneer.

Followers of the Nazarene have learned to analyze the pointedly positive, our ostensible thoughts and words, our external behavior, that is, to ask ourselves: What is behind my so-called positive aspects?
If we want to look the truth about ourselves in the eye, then we could apply the Ten Commandments of God and compare our hidden aspects with His commandments. Then we will

very soon notice what isn't in order, and know what needs to be done and how we should actually think, speak and act. This would be the guideline for a truly positive thinking.

You will rightly say: What is presented here cannot be proved. Why not? Because God wants you to prove to yourself that God lives in you. Followers of Jesus of Nazareth can talk about it, because many a one of us has had the profound experience: God, the power of life, in him, in all of us.
Life is eternal life because God is eternal. When you speak of life, think of the All-consciousness, God. Because He beheld and created you, all of us, in the very basis of our soul, we will live eternally as divine beings, as pure beings, that is, not as human beings.

Who doesn't know that at some point or other the physical body of each one passes on? But the Christ of God is present and He calls us as human beings. He calls the soul when it is discarnate, that is, when it has separated from its body. The call is: *Come to me, all who labor and are heavy-laden, and I – that is, Christ – will give you rest!*

To where should we turn, when many a sorrow or pain oppresses us, when our faith wavers or we do not believe in anything at all? At some point, the time comes when we ask: Is there a God?

If you ask this question, listen deep into the very basis of your soul and you will hear the call: *"Come to Me,"* thus speaks Christ, *"for I will give rest to all who labor and are heavy-laden!"*
The one who has practiced analysis and keeps his conscience alert and active will very quickly grasp the meaning of God's commandments and ultimately, of the Sermon on the Mount of Jesus, as well.

People of the New Era

Whether we believe it or not, a New Era has dawned. It is coming. Many a one wants to become a new person, a person of freedom, a person in the Spirit of God, a person who cherishes nature, who loves it and, with the strength of God, meets his neighbor in peace. These are the people of the New Era, of the coming generations. Will you join in?
You do not need external leaders. You have the inner leader, the Spirit of the Christ of God in you. He is in every one of us. Try finding your way to yourself, in order to grow closer to the true life! No one may force you to spiritual action. In the Spirit of truth, in God, you, all of us, are free people. No one must, but each one may!

What do we understand with the term true life? Anyone who, surrounded by many others, sees and hears himself will think: "I live!"

Let us again ask ourselves the deeper question: "Is our earthly life" – as we imagine it – "actually our true life?"

If you want to know more precisely what and how the true life looks, then simply take the Ten Commandments of God or the Sermon on the Mount of Jesus in hand. Read the words calmly and judiciously. A good analyst who strives to grasp the context of meaning of the clear statements looks deeper and understands what God, the Almighty, placed into the Ten Commandments, which He gave us through Moses.

A good analyst will also understand and recognize the depths of the Sermon on the Mount of Jesus. The true life is rooted in the depths. And the true life can be lived. It is given as guideline and offer to every person – when and if he wants it. In the process, we will not be religious highbrows or even holy. We become a calm, more judicious person, who simply and earnestly applies consciously the rule for life that Jesus of Nazareth taught us. It is: *Do to others as you would have them do to you.* A popular formulation of this instruction is: *Do not do to another what you do not want to have done to you.*

Basically, both statements amount to the same thing. You have to learn to understand them; you have to fathom them in their depths. If we have understood them, if we act according to them, step by step, then we will experience many a small so-called miracle, because it's going much better for us. We become happier and not lastly, freer. We no longer follow people and do not bind ourselves to any person. We feel and experience what freedom means.

A commandment of God is freedom. Who doesn't want it? And so, we try to analyze the commandments step by step, to understand the Sermon on the Mount and to apply it in our daily life! That's what brings freedom. That brings us close to God. From this, we learn: God in us. That is the true reality, the true life, which, despite the global decline in all spheres, despite negative developments and the suffering everywhere, lets us become glad again.

We, all of us, have one Father, the Father in heaven. Pray to His Spirit that dwells in you, in all of us. For God, our Father, loves every single one of us. His love is inviolable and indelible.

Through our heart prayers, we grow close to Him, the eternal Father, and experience His power and help in us. We learn that we people do not need church denominations, or church traditions. Basically, the priests are also superfluous, because we do not need intercessors.

We have something wonderful, something un-equaled in us, a treasure, an unimaginably valuable treasure.

We are called upon by Jesus, the Christ, to un-earth this treasure in us, because Jesus taught us: *I,* that is, Christ, *Am the way, the truth and the life.* And He, Christ, asked us to follow Him, that is, Christ. Ultimately, for all of us, this means to seek out the quiet chamber, to pray and to put into practice the truths that open up to us in deep prayer.

God is present

It is a great gift that we may have the experience: God in us.

So, in time, you will realize that you become freer and happier. You will then notice that everything external, for instance, seeking God in stone churches is all theory.

Set out to unearth this one-of-a-kind treasure and you will gain the joy of being close to someone in your heart. Of course, it is not a person, nothing external – you draw closer to the One whom we address as "Our Father" in the Lord's Prayer, *Our Father who are in heaven, hallowed is Your name.*

Hallow His name! Pray into the very basis of your soul. Pray deeply and fulfill your prayers, step by step, and you will notice that someone is there, the Father in heaven, who is praised in the Lord's Prayer. Soon you will sense that you are not alone, that something knocks and beats, breathes and flows. You feel that it is the Spirit; it is the Spirit of our heavenly Father, the truth. It is the flow of life in you, in all of us.

How close the quiet chamber comes to us! You achieve certainty, because in time your prayers become deeper, because the freedom grows and you meet the innermost part of your fellow humans in a completely new way. The inner happiness, which has grown in you and continues to grow, radiates and can touch the soul of your fellow humans, provided they are also searching to find God, the true God. Let us once more bring to mind the message, which, when we become aware of it, grants us ever more inner security, and in our daily life, brings us the incomparable certainty of being carried by the divine All-power and love. You do not need external leaders. You have the best leader – *in* you. It is the inner leader,

the Spirit of infinity, the Christ of God in the
very basis of your soul.

> He is in you; He is in us –
> He is always present.
>
> When you go for a walk –
> God is present.
>
> When you talk with your fellow
> people – God is present.
>
> When you are at work –
> God is present.
>
> When you dine –
> God is present.
>
> When you go to bed –
> God is present.
>
> When you awaken –
> God is present.
>
> He, the mighty Spirit in you,
> wants to go with you into the day.

Dear fellow people, what better could we wish
for than peace, joy, happiness, health, and
not lastly, God with us, because God is in us!

You need not go here
or there — I Am in you!
And wherever you are, I Am there.
Withdraw to a quiet chamber and
go into the little chamber of your heart,
to pray from your heart.
In prayer, bring your heart's concerns
to Me, who has taken up dwelling in you,
and believe that I can do everything.

Christ in
"This Is My Word. Alpha and Omega.
The Gospel of Jesus.
The Christ-Revelation, which True Christians
the World Over Have Come to Know"

Read also ...

This is My Word
A and Ω

The Gospel of Jesus
The Christ-Revelation which true Christians the world over have come to know

This encompassing Christ-Revelation goes way beyond the contents of the Bible. This great work gives an overall picture of what was, of what is – and of what will be.

Building on the "Gospel of Jesus," an existing extra-biblical gospel text, Christ Himself reveals through Gabriele, the prophetess and emissary of God, details of His incarnation in Jesus of Nazareth.

From the contents: Childhood and Youth of Jesus • The Falsification of the Teaching of Jesus of Nazareth over the past 2000 years • Purpose and Meaning of Life on Earth • Jesus taught the law of cause and effect • Prerequisites for the healing of the body •Jesus taught about marriage • God does not rage and punish • The teaching of "eternal damnation" is a mockery of God • Jesus exposed scribes and Pharisees as hypocrites • Jesus loved the animals and always spoke up for them • About death, reincarnation and life • The true meaning of the Redeemer Deed of Christ ... and much, much more...

with a short autobiography of Gabriele

1078 pp., softbd, Order No. S 007en, ISBN: 978-1-890841-38-6. $ 15.00

Also available as an E-Book for only $ 3.40
(www.this-is-my-word.com)

Excerpts are also available: www.gabriele-publishing-house.com

The Speaking All-Unity

The Word of the Universal Creator-Spirit

A Cosmic Work of Teaching and Learning from the School of Divine Wisdom

Taken from conversations with Gabriele, compiled by Martin Kübli and Ulrich Seifert

Have you always had the feeling of being connected to a higher power, but not to any religion? Because the teachings were inconsistent, because your questions were not answered or because the religious words and the deeds did not appear to be in accord?

This books will make it possible for you to develop a new image of God. From the Big Bang to the question of why there are addictions, murder and natural disasters, you will find answers to the questions which denominational teachings leave unanswered.

Learn why the respectful and loving treatment of other beings of life is so important, about what we can learn from the animals and how we can live in harmony with nature. And, find out how you, too, can develop a more conscious life: with knowledge, a respectful and loving way of seeing things, meditations, and practice.

Includes an Audio-CD with two meditations:

1. "Everything Is in Bloom" – a meditative virtual walk

2. "Our True Being" – a meditative cosmic view

382 pp., hardbd., many fotos, Order No. S 173en
ISBN:978-1-890841-33-1, $ 29.00

Learn to Pray

In True Prayer You Experience God.
True Prayer Makes You Happy

God dwells in the soul of each person. So He is always very close to us. He listens to us and understands us. Every person can learn to speak with Him in prayer. The book, "Learn to Pray," written by Gabriele, gives instructions on the free prayer that is also carried by our feelings and leads us, in the end, to the prayer of the deed.

56 pp., softbd., Order No. S 174en, ISBN: 978-1-890841-74-4, $4.00

Free Broschures

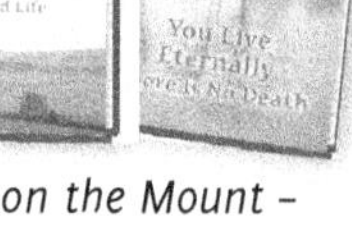

* Pearls of Life for You
* You Are Not Alone
* You Live eternally –
  There Is No Death
* A Fulfilled Life into Old Age
* Help for the Sick and Suffering
* Find God! Where? How?

* The Sermon on the Mount –
  The Path to a Fulfilled Life
* Don't Let Go!
* Reincarnation –
  Life's Gift of Grace
* The Suffering of Animals
  Is the Grave of Mankind

www.ingramcontent.com/pod-product-compliance
Lightning Source LLC
LaVergne TN
LVHW051106180726
843512LV00020B/1634